# Reading
# for
# Ourselves

**Sarah Crowley**

**Oxfam**
UK and Ireland

A catalogue record for this book is available from the British Library

ISBN 0 35598 201 2

Front cover photograph *El Salvador: refugees from the civil war organised literacy classes for themselves while they were in exile in Honduras. Now, like this woman in Ciudad Segundo Montes, they are rebuilding their lives back home in their own country.*
Jenny Matthews/Oxfam

Published by Oxfam, 274 Banbury Road, Oxford OX2 7DZ
Designed and typeset by Oxfam Design Department NY61/PK/93
Set in 11/14pt Garamond
Printed by Oxfam Print Unit on environment-friendly paper

# Contents

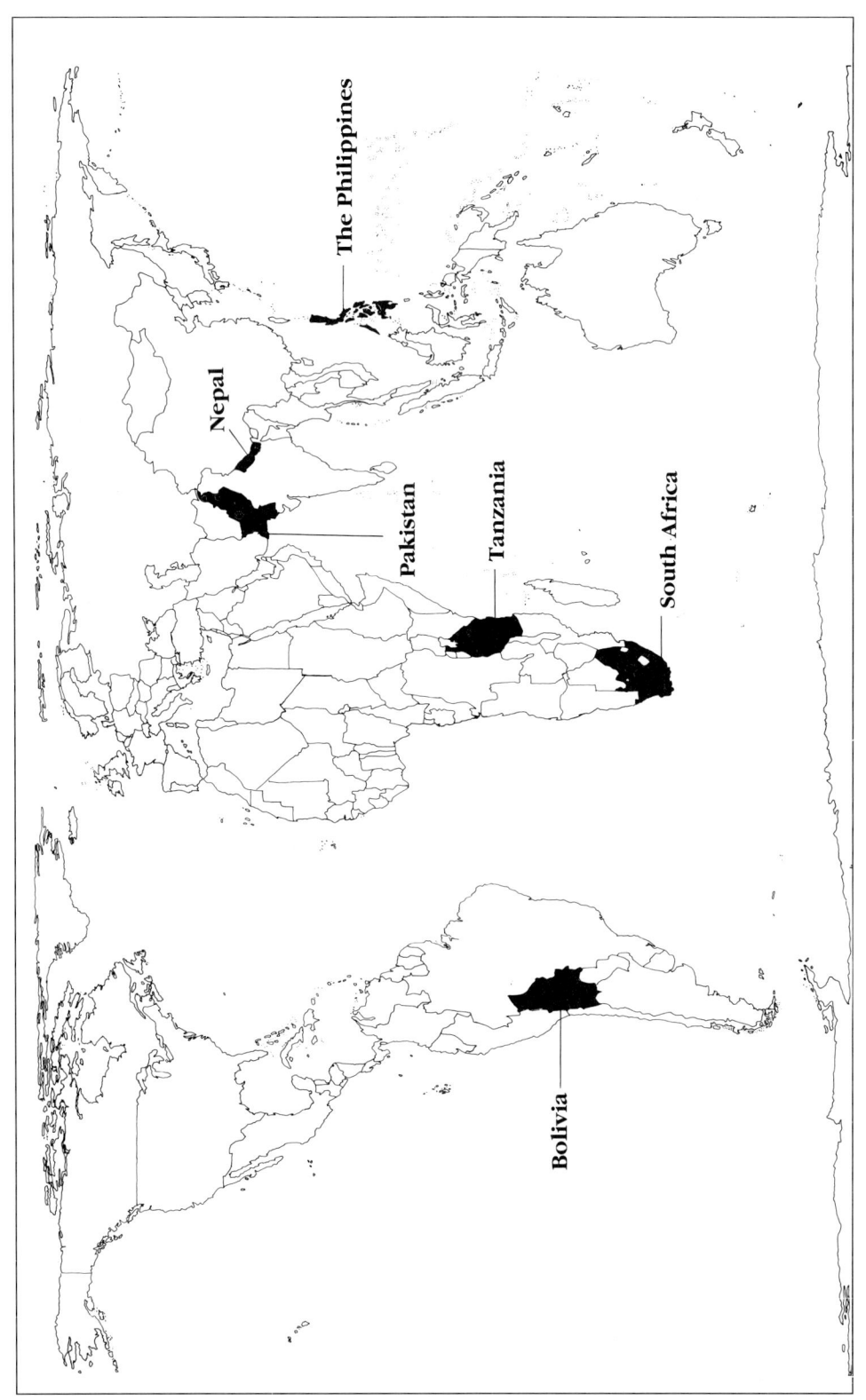

The Philippines

Nepal

Pakistan

Tanzania

South Africa

Bolivia

**A Peters Projection map of the world, showing the countries featured in this book**

# Foreword

The United Kingdom is a long way from the countries described in this book — Bolivia, Nepal, Pakistan, the Philippines, South Africa, and Tanzania. Life for poor people in distant countries like these is very different from life in countries like the United Kingdom.

But people all over the world need to learn to read, write, and calculate. And if they did not learn at school when they were young, or if they never went to school, they face problems which are much the same in every country.

Selina, in South Africa, describes in this book how she could not write down messages when she worked in a hotel. In the UK, too, many people (especially women) who work in low-paid jobs, cleaning or caring for other people, find it hard to write things down.

Women in Manila, capital of the Philippines, go to classes "because we want to know more". Being able to read gives them confidence in themselves. In Pakistan, people want to read because they don't like having to ask other people to read their private letters for them. In Nepal, people want to learn so that they won't be cheated by money-lenders. In the UK, people go to literacy classes for all these reasons.

It takes courage and energy for people to go to classes and learn new things. In this book, we see women in Nepal walking for half an hour at the end of a hard day to attend evening classes. In Bolivia the old people's eyesight is bad and their fingers are so stiff that they can hardly hold a pencil. But they are determined to learn. There is so little money for the classes that they have to break the pencils in half and share them. In the UK, people face the same sorts of problem.

In Britain, there has been education for everyone for more than 100 years. But that does not mean that everyone found it easy to learn, or easy to feel good about themselves. Too many people — especially women — learned that what they have to say does not matter. Like the women in the Tanzanian village described in this book, they get the confidence to speak out and stand up for themselves when they get better at reading and writing.

The places in this book are very far away. But now — thanks to the stories told here — some of them are a little closer.

*Jane Mace*
*Senior Lecturer in Community Education,*
*Goldsmiths' College, London*
*May 1993*

1

# Nepal:
# "Now people can't cheat us"

Nepal is a beautiful country
north of India.
There are many mountains.
The villages up there
are very isolated.
The people speak
a language called Nepali,
which is like Hindi.
The girls often don't go to school,
because they are needed at home
to help their mothers
with their work.

In the villages
the women have a lot of work to do.
Some women have to walk
down a steep hill
to get all their water.
They carry it in pots
on their backs with a strap
that goes round their foreheads.
The women do all the work in the home.
They cook on stoves which burn wood.
They have to collect the wood.
They look after the children.
They also have to look after
goats, cows, and chickens,
and they grow vegetables.
The men share in the farming work.

The only time the women can go
to reading and writing classes
is in the evenings after dark.
Some women live half an hour's walk
away from the class.
They meet in a barn
that is cold in winter.
The only light they have
is a paraffin lamp.
The classes are free.
They meet six evenings a week.

The women who go to the class
have had no chance to go to school.
They go because they want
to help their children.
They also want to be able to read,
so they won't be cheated
by the money-lenders.

*Nepal: cooking the evening meal in Chepater
village, near Gorkha.*
(Jeremy Hartley/Oxfam)

An Oxfam worker called Rita
visited the group.
She asked the women
what they felt about the classes.
They said,
"Before, we were in darkness.
Now we have seen the light."
They sang a song before she left
in which they said:
"Give us education and we won't fail.
We'll be able to manage our lives in future."

The teacher is a woman
from the village.
She has had some education.
In the class they discuss things
that are important in their lives
like health, forests, and agriculture.

They invite government officials
to the classes
to talk about these things.
The women ask them questions.
The women say that
before they went to classes
they would not have dared
to speak to people
who work for the government.
Speaking to the women
also helps the officials
to understand
the needs of the village.

All the women enjoy the classes
because they get a chance to meet
and talk with other women.

Right — *Nepal:
cutting grass for
cattle-food. The
Himalayan
mountain range
is in the back-
ground.*
(Jeremy Hartley/
Oxfam)

Below — *Nepal:
women thresh-
ing rice.*
(Jeremy Hartley/
Oxfam)

# Tanzania:
# Doing the accounts and making a profit

Naisinyai is a Maasai village in Tanzania. It is on the plains below Mount Kilimanjaro. A few years ago the people decided they wanted to improve life in the village. They knew that health care was very important. Health-care classes were started at the church. It was mostly women who went. They learned how to prevent illnesses like malaria, and they set up a health committee. In the classes the women were encouraged to say what was important to them. They began to speak out in village meetings.

The health committee saw that shortage of milk was a problem in the village. More than half the calves were dying from East Coast Fever. The men said they should spray the cattle. The women said they should build a cattle dip, because that would use less chemicals. The health committee voted and, because there were more women than men, they decided to get a cattle dip. Mr Kisota, the chair of the village council, told an Oxfam worker called Geoff: "The men thought the women were wasting their time, continually discussing the dip, but when the women came to a decision, you could be sure that something would happen."

Oxfam gave them the building materials, and everyone in the village helped to build the dip. The women buy the chemicals in 200-litre drums. Every four litres of chemical are diluted by 4,000 litres of water from the river. The cattle

Tanzania: Mrs Kisota practises writing her signature, watched by Paulina, a worker with the Maasai Health Services Project. Mrs Kisota is preparing to open a bank account on behalf of the women's cattle-dip project. (Geoff Sayer/Oxfam)

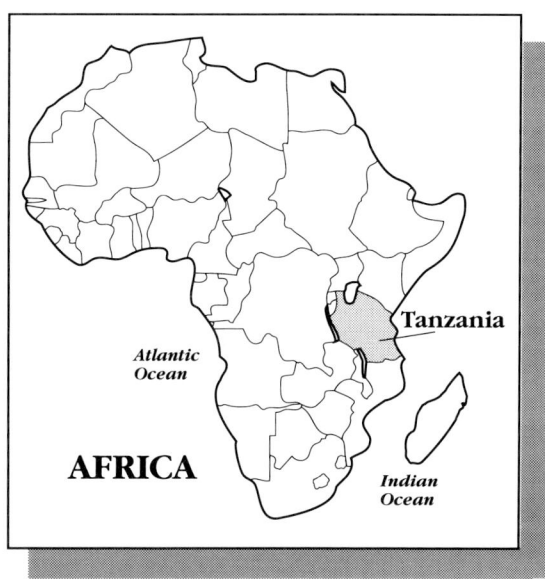

owners have to pay five Tanzanian shillings* for each cow that goes through the dip. This covers the cost and also gives the villagers a small profit, which they can use to develop other projects for the village. The village council has passed a law to say that all the cattle have to be dipped every week. About 1,000 cattle go through the dip each day, and the dip is in use four days a week. People from other villages bring their cattle to the dip as well.

In 1989 the women of Naisinyai bought the first 200-litre drum of chemicals with a loan from the village. The drum cost 56,000 shillings. The nearest place to buy the chemicals was Kibaya, the district capital, 200 kilometres away. The transport costs were 10,000 shillings. The income from this first drum was 108,000 shillings.

*Maria Mtero, a member of the women's group, talking at a village meeting.*
(Geoff Sayer/Oxfam)

5

The second drum cost 70,000, but the transport was cheaper: 4,500. This time the village lent them 33,000 shillings, and the income was 100,000. The third drum cost 74,000 shillings, and again the transport costs were 4,500; the income was 100,000. The fourth drum cost 90,000 shillings, and the chemicals were transported free by health workers visiting the village. By this time the women were beginning to make a profit and had paid off their loans from the village.

The women decided they wanted to do their own accounts for the dip. They said, "We're not having the men keeping our accounts. Men are hopeless with money." This meant that they needed numeracy classes. Paulina, one of the health workers, began to train them in book-keeping. As soon as the dip made a profit, they had to open a bank account for the first time. They had to practise signing their names and filling in forms. Some of the women had been to school when they were young, but they hadn't used reading, writing, or numeracy since, so they had forgotten a lot of it.

The women were worried about taking the money home at night. They were not afraid of being robbed. They thought that if it was known who had taken the money home, that woman's husband would put pressure on her to lend him the money. He might say it was needed for other village business like mending the lorry. The women decided that the safest way was for all of them to carry home a bag every night, so no one would know who really had the money.

Since the women set up the cattle dip, East Coast Fever has almost disappeared. The women now feel much more confident. There is a lot of support and friendship between them. But they still face many problems. All their water comes from a dirty river. If they had a borehole, they would have clean water. They are thinking of using money from the cattle dip to pay for a borehole and for pipes to deliver clean water round the village. They would also like a dispensary, to provide the village with simple medicines.

Maria Mteru, one of the women involved in the dip, said to Geoff, "We're proud of our village and what we've achieved."

* In 1990 when Geoff visited the village, the monthly income from the dip was 57,000 shillings. At that time there were 345 shillings to the pound sterling. Five shillings bought one banana. Sugar cost 100 a kilo. A daily newspaper cost 40. A teacher or a nurse earned about 2,000 shillings a month. The Maasai people earn money by selling cattle, milk, and hides.

*Maria Mtero at the cattle-dip in Naisinyai.*
(Geoff Sayer/Oxfam)

# Bolivia:
# "I've always wanted to sign my name"

La Paz is the capital of Bolivia. Around the edges of the city are shanty towns, where the very poorest people live. Many people who live there have difficulty with reading and writing.

One organisation runs 63 adult education groups in the city. All the teachers are volunteers who live in the shanty towns.

In one place there are 80 women who meet in the open air. They sit on the stony ground to learn. The women are divided into different groups. Some of them went to school when they were young, so they can learn more quickly. There are food shortages and health problems in the area, so they read about these issues and discuss them.

One group is called the Grandmothers' Group. They are older women who never went to school. They are taught by Carolina, who is 16. She goes to school in the mornings. On

Tuesday afternoons she teaches reading and writing. Many of the older women have problems learning. They can't see well and their fingers are very stiff, so it is hard to hold a pencil.

Juana Monroy is 62. She says, "I have never been to school. In my time, parents used to say, 'Studying is for boys, the girls can't go'. That's why I never learned. Now my eyesight is bad, I can't read. But I've always wanted to sign my name." Carolina says, "You need a lot of patience to start from scratch at their age, but we have fun."

In another group there is a student called Justa Quista. She has five children. She says, "It is difficult for us to get time off to come here. My husband says, 'Why are you going to waste

*Bolivia: a literacy class in La Paz.*
(Sean Sprague/Oxfam)

your time there? You are too old to learn. It will make your head spin.' I just tell him, 'Look, I'm going for a bit of a break. I get fed up at home with the kids and problems and all.' "

These classes are only once a week. There is very little money for pencils and paper. They break the pencils in half, so more people can have one. There are not many books.

In Bolivia the official language is Spanish, but the people who go to these classes speak Aymara. Aymara was spoken in Bolivia before the Spanish arrived. These literacy groups have chosen to learn to read in Spanish, because they say it is more useful. They say they can't stand up for themselves if they don't know Spanish.

One of the teachers is called Sonia. She says, "There are lots of women who want to learn, but people have such bad financial problems, they have to give up the chance to study, and go for whatever will fill their families' stomachs."

The students say they go to classes "So we won't be cheated" ... "So we won't have to say that we don't know how to sign our names" ... "So we can help our kids with their home-work" ... "So we'll know who to vote for".

*Bolivia: grandmothers learning to read and write at a literacy class in La Paz.*
(Jenny Matthews/Oxfam)

9

# The Philippines:
# A chance to meet and talk

Manila is the capital city
of the Philippines.
Tondo is a slum area of the city.
The houses are huts on stilts
in the waters of Manila Bay.
It is very crowded
and often there are floods.
People reach their homes
by paths over big rocks.
The people here are very poor.
There are few services
and no electricity.

There is a women's
reading and writing class in Tondo.
Oxfam pays for the teacher.
She is called Emma Orozco.
About 12 women go to the class.
They are all aged over 50.
There was no school for them
when they were children.
They go to the class
because they feel
they want to know more.
They can't read
where the bus is going to.

These women spend a lot of their time
looking after their own children
and their grandchildren.
They make some money
by selling food or sewing.
They are very pleased to go to the class.
It gives them a chance to meet and talk.

The classroom is tiny.
There is a blackboard.
They meet two or three times a week
during the day.
They can't meet at night,
because it's not safe for them to go out.
Also there is no light to read by.

*Negros Island, the Philippines: workers at
a demonstration demand 'Equal Pay For
Women and Men'.*
(Belinda Coote/Oxfam)

10

They read from a book
which they wrote themselves.
They also discuss problems
that affect them,
like poor health care and prostitution.
They enjoy going to the class.
They are very proud of being able to learn.
They feel more confident now.

*The Philippines: Mrs Flor David, a community health worker, tells women in a shanty town how to stop their children getting tetanus.*
(Nancy Durrell-McKenna/Oxfam)

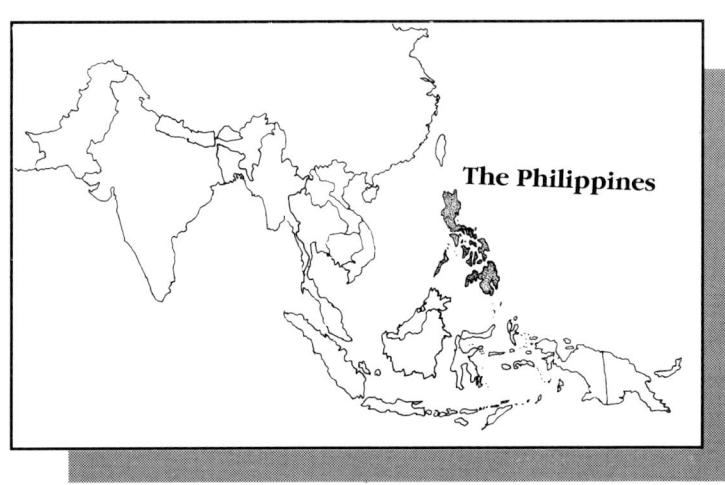

**The Philippines**

# *Pakistan:*
# Reading the signs

The Nai Roshni school
is in a city called Quetta.
Quetta is in the west of Pakistan,
near the border with Afghanistan.
There are mountains
all round the city.

The area round the school
has steep narrow streets.
There are no pavements.
The streets have drains
running down both sides.
There are little bridges to cross
to get to the shops.

An Oxfam worker,
Mohammed Ali Gulzari,
lives in this part of the city.
He lives with his mother,
his brothers, his wife,
and his children.
Their home is like many
in the area.
It has two rooms.
Outside there is
a covered kitchen
and a toilet.
There is no running water.
They get water
from a tap outside
in their yard.
In the rooms are thin mattresses.

They sit on these
during the day and
sleep on them at night.
When they eat, they put
a tablecloth on the floor.
They have a TV.

The Nai Roshni school
is for adult women and girls.
The women missed out
on education
when they were young.

The girls work
in the handicraft industry
and go to the school
in the evening.

There are 33 women
in the literacy class.
Six of them are Afghan refugees.
Most of them
are in their twenties.
A few of them are married.

They study literacy and numeracy.
They learn about health in a class
with some of the older girls
in the school.
They also have some time each week
when they discuss the problems
they face in their lives.

Farzana is divorced.
She has a 10-year-old child.
She is going to the class
to learn numeracy,
in order to get a job.
She can sew and embroider,
but the handicraft centre
won't employ her
unless she can add up figures.
If she had a job,
she would be less dependent
on her family.

Zahra's husband is working
in Kuwait for a year.
When he wrote letters to her,
she decided she needed
to learn to read.
She had to ask other people
to read her letters for her.
She didn't like other people
knowing her business.

*Pakistan: street signs in Urdu and English in the city of Karachi.*
(Ben Buxton/Oxfam)

An Oxfam worker called Sabrina
visited the class.
When she talked to the women,
they said to her
that being unable to read
is a form of blindness.
It is a real disability for them.
They can't read road signs.
When they go shopping,
they can't read the shop signs
or the prices.
They would like to be able
to read cooking instructions
on food packets.
Some women want to read
what programmes are on the TV.

# South Africa:
# "I can read it on my own"

The Bulamahlo Learning Project in South Africa is funded by Oxfam. It is based in Shiluvane, which is a black settlement in a homeland in the Transvaal. Under *apartheid* the homelands were created as separate areas for the blacks to live in. This left most of the good land for the whites.

The area is very poor and overcrowded. Some people are employed on the farms owned by whites more than 50 miles away. They have to leave home at 4.00 in the morning and don't get home till 7.00 or 8.00 at night. Mostly it is the men who work on the farms.

There are 94 literacy groups in the area. The teaching is in Sotho, the local language. Some people learn English when they have learnt to read and write Sotho. Each student has three two-hour classes a week. The classes are free, but they have to buy their own books.

*South Africa: an open-air class in Shiluvane, Transvaal.*
(Matthew Sherrington/Oxfam)

An Oxfam worker called Matthew went to visit a class in 1992. He spoke to two students, Miriam Komana and Selina Mailula.

Miriam Komana was born in 1941. She is a widow with six children. She used to work on a farm, but lost her job. Then she worked in a school kitchen. Now she says, "I am not old enough to get a pension, so I buy fruit and vegetables from white farms and sell them in the market." Three mornings a week she has to go in search of firewood.

When she was young, Miriam didn't go to school. She had to work on the farm. "In those days people did not think that young girls should go to school." Miriam says she always wanted to learn to read. She didn't like asking other people to read her letters. She also wanted to read the Bible in church. What finally made her start classes was a trip to the Post Office. "My brother sent me something from Johannesburg and at the Post Office I had to sign. I was very embarrassed to just put an X."

Miriam has been going to classes for three years. She feels confident about her reading, but her writing is not very good yet. She works hard. "In the evening I sit with a candle and work at what we have done in the day, so that I can understand it."

As Miriam was speaking to Matthew ouside the class, someone called over the fence

to her. A letter had come from her daughter. She opened it and smiled. "Now I am happy, because I can read it on my own."

Selina Mailula has been going to classes for six months. She was born in 1963 and has two children aged 11 and 1. Her husband works in a liquor store 60 miles away. He comes home only once or twice a month.

Selina didn't go to school, because her mother was a single parent and could not afford the fees. Not being able to read and write has caused her many problems. "I worked in a white farmer's house for six years. If I answered the phone when no one was at home, I

could never take a message, because I couldn't write. I couldn't even write down the phone number for the baas." (Baas is a black South African name for a white boss.) Later she worked in a hotel. Sometimes she had to help out in the hotel shop. That was difficult too. "There were things I could not do, like registering goods and reading the prices."

Now her husband goes away to work, she has other problems. "Sometimes he sends me money, and I didn't know how to sign for it at the Post Office. And when he wrote letters I had to ask friends to read them for me. They know all my secrets. Sometimes I even had to pay people to sign for my money or read my letters."

It took Selina a while to persuade her husband to let her go to classes. "He went to school and can read, but when I wanted to start last year, we were building our house. He said that the classes weren't important and that I should look after the children. He thought the classes were all day and that I wouldn't work in the house."

When the house was finished, Selina asked her husband again. He said she could go to the class. "Now he is very happy that I am learning. For the first months we learned letters, then how to write our names." Her mother looks after the baby while she is at class.

Selina studies as much as she can when she has done her house work. She borrows children's books from the school. "My son helps sometimes if I get it wrong." Her husband encourages her to read the Bible.

After six months she still finds reading difficult. With help she can read her husband's letters. She can also sign her name to get money at the Post Office. "I can read road signs and signs on houses like 'Beware of the dog'!" she laughs.

Selina would like to become a teacher, "to share this cleverness with others". She knows that more women than men have problems with reading and writing. "It is important for women to read and write, so they can do things on their own and not rely on others. I feel more confident now."

*South Africa: time to relax at a literacy class in Soweto.*
(Nancy Durrell-McKenna/Oxfam)

# Resources list

## Background reading

The following books, published by Oxfam for adults, give more information about life in some of the countries featured in *Reading for Ourselves*.

### Bolivia
*The Andes: A Quest for Justice*, by Neil MacDonald (1992)*

### Nepal
*Nepal: A Country Profile*, by Omar Sattaur (due March 1994)*

### Pakistan
*Pakistan: A Country Profile*, by Khavar Mumtaz (due December 1993)*

### The Philippines
*The Philippines: Debt and Poverty*, by Rosalinda Pineda-Ofreneo (1991)*

### South Africa
*We Cry For Our Land: Farm Workers in South Africa*, by Wendy Davies (1990)*

### General
*Half the World, Half a Chance: An Introduction to Gender and Development*, by Julia Cleves Mosse (1992)

## Resources for teachers

The following resources (published by Oxfam or with support from Oxfam) include activities for teaching about the countries featured in *Reading for Ourselves*. They are designed for use with children and young people, but can be adapted for use with adults.

### Pakistan
*Gariyan: Transport in Pakistan* (Oxfam, 1992)**

### Tanzania
*Hanging by a Thread*: explores issues of trade and debt, using cotton production in Tanzania as a case study (Leeds DEC, 1992)**

*New Journeys*: explores themes of tourism, self-reliance, and land use in Kenya and Tanzania (Birmingham DEC, 1992)**

*Living and Learning in a Tanzanian Village*: a case study of Kirua Primary School (Manchester DEP, 1992)**

### South Africa
*Art Against Apartheid* (Art and Development Education Project, 1990)**

*The Kei Road Eviction*: a role-play activity based on a real-life incident when farm workers were evicted from their homes (Oxfam, 1990)**

### The Philippines
*Here and Davao*: photos, activities, and interviews about life in the Philippines (available from Newcastle Development Education Unit)***

### General
*Right to Read*: activities to illustrate literacy issues, with case studies (available from Leeds DEC, 1993)***

*Oxfam Peters Projection Map* (Oxfam Publications, 1989)*

* Available from Oxfam Publications Department, 274 Banbury Road, Oxford OX2 7DZ (tel. 0865 311311). Publications catalogue sent on request.

** Available from Oxfam Young People's Team, 274 Banbury Road, Oxford OX2 7DZ (tel. 0865 311311). Education catalogue sent on request.

*** Available from the publishers; addresses are given in the Oxfam Education catalogue (available from the Young People's Team at the above address).

# Oxfam and Literacy

Oxfam supports many more literacy and numeracy groups around the world, like the ones described in this booklet.

Millions of adults in the world cannot read or write. Many of them missed the chance to go to school when they were young, because they live in poor countries which cannot afford to educate everybody.

If people can't read, they don't know what their legal rights are. In Bangladesh, for example, landless people are allowed to claim empty land, to grow food for their families. But often they don't know how to claim the land, and rich people take it instead. So Oxfam pays for teachers and books and pencils, to help the landless people to learn to read.

If people can't read and write, they can't open a bank account. They have to borrow from money lenders, who charge very high rates of interest. Some of the people in the literacy classes in Bangladesh now have bank accounts. Others have set up their own village savings groups, to raise money for community projects.

---

*On the Atlantic Coast of Nicaragua, people speak English and Spanish. Here a woman in the town of Bluefields reads 'Sunrise', a bi-lingual community newspaper funded by Oxfam.*
(Mike Goldwater/Oxfam)

If people can't do sums, they can't set up their own businesses. In Senegal, village women have to support their families when the men go off to find work in the towns. Oxfam is helping women to learn to read and do sums. They built their own classrooms. Now some have opened a shop, selling things like soap; others are selling smoked fish in the market.

If women can't read, they can't find out about family planning methods, and they can't read the words on medicine bottles when their children are ill. In Kenya, health workers decided to start classes in literacy for local women. Oxfam pays the

teachers. The women and the teachers are writing their own books. The first word that the women learned to read was *kame*, which means 'mother'.

If people can't read, and they get separated from each other, they sometimes forget their own history and culture. On the east coast of Nicaragua, in a very isolated area, Oxfam funds a community newspaper called *Sunrise*. It keeps people in touch with each other, and it records their stories of the old times. Oxfam helped to pay for the printing press and office equipment.

Oxfam set up a Literacy Fund in 1992, to raise money for more  projects like these. Money comes from public contributions; royalties from books published by Oxfam with other publishers; special promotions with publishers or booksellers; and 'bring and buy' book sales organised by schools, libraries, and other groups.

The Oxfam Literacy Fund links people who can read in the countries of the North with those who are struggling for the power that literacy brings in the poor countries of the South. For more details, contact The Oxfam Literacy Fund, Oxfam, 274 Banbury Road, Oxford OX2 7DZ.

*Nicaragua: After the revolution in 1979, 95,000 students, factory workers, and civil servants volunteered to run literacy classes in poor communities. In six months, over 400,000 Nicaraguans had learned to read and write. Oxfam helped to fund this Literacy Crusade.*
(Mike Goldwater/Oxfam)